Places We Could Never Find Alone

Places We Could Never Find Alone

Millard Dunn

INK
BRUSH
PRESS

ISBN: 978-0-9827514-8-0
Library of Congress Control Number: 2011925295

Manufactured in the United States

Ink Brush Press
Temple, Texas

Acknowledgments

The author gratefully acknowledges the following publications in which versions of these poems appeared, sometimes with different titles:

Arable: "Artificial Insemination Clinic"
Concho River Review: "Been There, Done That"; "Sex Education"
Film and History: "Sands of Iwo Jima"
Hard Scuffle Folio: "Pigs in the Sun"; "Feeding Pigs"; "The Smell of Pigs"; "Pigs in Cold Weather"
The IUS Review: "Picasso's Late Drawings"
Jam To-Day: "Making an Impression"; "Lavoisier's Diamond"
Kansas Quarterly: "Directions"; "But She's Not You"; "Hunting Frogs"
The Louisville Review: "Kate's Birthday, Falling This Year on the Day We Change Times"; "My Tongue, waiting for your tongue"; "Ferris Wheel"; "Map Fragment, on Clay"; "For the Gas Men"; "Values of Fundamental Constants Adjusted"; "Prairie Lighthouse"; "Dragon"; "Engraved on Air"
New North Carolina Poetry, The Eighties: "Sunday Night: the Youth Fellowship"; "Monday Night: The Preacher"
The Ohio Review: "Sleeping with Bees"
Poetry Northwest: "Choirmaster"
The Sandhills, St. Andrews Review: "The sound of rain carries memory where it will"; "The Forgotten Child"
Southern Poetry Review: "Jean Louise at the Ninth Grade Prom"
this end up postcards: "Map Fragment, on Clay"

The following poems appeared in my chapbook *Engraved On Air* (The Kentucky Arts Council and The Kentucky Department for Libraries and Archives, 1983): "Siren"; "My Tongue, Waiting for Your Tongue"; "Ferris Wheel"; "Map Fragment, on Clay"; "Directions"; "Courtly Love"; "Your First Lover"; "Dragon"; "Pigs in the Sun"; "Engraved on Air"; "Choirmaster"; "Monday Night: The Preacher"; "Tuesday Night: the Old Folks"; "Wednesday Night: Newlyweds"; "Saturday Night: the Dead"; and "First Words"

I am grateful to The National Endowment for the Humanities, The Kentucky Foundation for Women, The Kentucky Arts Council, and Indiana University Southeast for their generous support during the writing of these poems.

For Carole

CONTENTS

More Than Adequate to Any Task

Places We Could Never Find Alone

Our Lives, Volcanic, Wait Our Waking

Terra Incognita

Family Suidae, Genus Sus, Species domestica

Carolina Gospel Old-Time Revival Week

Taking On Knowledge

Directed by the Wind and Sun

More Than Adequate to Any Task

For the Gas Men

Every day they are in the street
cutting through the asphalt.
Their air hammer sounds like

a thousand sheep, very hungry
screaming right in your ear,
following you everywhere. Close

the windows. You cannot get away.
In the street they have cut precise
squares out of the pavement,

like lifting squares from the center
of a pan of brownies.
Amazing, that all the noise and dust,

the rounded blade of the air hammer,
cut so clean. "Sealing joints in the main,"
one of them tells you, very politely.

You wish you had that much faith,
to cut into anything, into your
day, your lover, your children, making

that much noise, knowing
beneath your own neat square incision
you could find the main, and seal it.

Holding a Course

Accurate means different things at different times,
and close is sometimes good enough. Take,
for example, John, a brick mason from South
Africa, who sailed single-handed across
the Atlantic. In an Annapolis bar he told
his story to a room full of racing sailors.
How did you steer at night? "Bungee cord
on the tiller." *How close a course?* "Give
or take thirty degrees." For these sailors,
in an ocean race one degree off course
could cost them the whole race. "All of South
America was waiting for me. I turned right
and sailed north. As long as I've got my trowel,
I can find a job." *Can you lay block
as well as brick?* "I can lay anything.
The trick is knowing how to hold a straight
course when you have to. And," he added,
"knowing when you have to."

Saturday Mornings at the Movies

Time and the real world, a celluloid
calculus that trapped them both, or so
we thought. Lurking in the dark, time past,
time future, time imagined become
time present, and we are there, dreaming
without knowing that we dream. Control
belongs to someone else, who long ago
left for another time. So who're you
going to believe, me or your own eyes?
Light loves to play: with time, with the world,
and lets us believe we know the game.
But light makes up the rules and directs
herself. We have been misinformed.

Watering the Lawn

July: the sprinklers
Simulate for grass
The rain that April
Gave abundantly.
My neighbor's two girls
Play in the water.
He says to them once,
Then says it again,
"Girls, you're getting my
Stuff wet." Time sits with
Me, waiting, while they
Play unfettered. Now
Is all that matters.
His stuff, we both know,
All his stuff, is doomed.

John Muir in Bonaventure Cemetery, October, 1867

The eagles wake him up. Every morning
They scream, hunting high over the river.
He lies still and stares into the faces
Of a crowd, small birds, staring back.

He has walked from Louisville, seven hundred
Miles, and is waiting in Savannah for
Money from his brother in Wisconsin.
He promised his mother he would sleep indoors

If he could. By now he can't afford
A room, and closer to town he is afraid.
For some here the war's not over, for many,
Not done for. He knows no one will bother him

In a cemetery after dark, and walks
The three or four miles out of town. That first
Night he sleeps under a live oak, a small mound
His pillow. In the morning it is a grave.

In a hidden thicket, he builds a small hut:
Bushes for corners, roof of rushes, a thick
Floor of Spanish moss to sleep on. He loves
The live oaks. Their twisted arms reach overhead,

Touch tree to tree, and create a tangled nave.
Gray moss hangs like graceful banners. By day
He studies Savannah's gardens. The genesis
Of this long walk, Kentucky to Florida,

Is botany, which in Savannah saves him.
When the money comes, a post office clerk
Refuses to hand it over. "How do I
Know you are John Muir?" "My brother's letter

Indicates I am a botanist. A thief
Could steal the letter, but not John Muir's
Knowledge of botany. Question me about
Any plant or tree." And he gets the money.

Our Parents' Hands

Levers in the joints and tendons and muscles
make our hands the lovely instruments
we live our lives depending on, and, as
we get older most of us never have—
not ever having looked—taken the chance
to compare our hands to the hands of our mothers
or fathers. And so I am moved to hear
you quote your mother, "I had always hoped
you would have your father's hands, those long
fingers, and all," and the implication
from your mother that you had inherited
her hands instead. Thus we imagine
together how he might have touched her, how
his long fingers as skillful as when he
sent code at forty words a minute
might have brought her comfort or joy, all
their years together. For myself, I remember
my father's hands as he baptized a child, holding
the infant on his shoulder, his hand all
bones, back and fingers wet from the font,
covering the crown of the child's head as if
it were fragile and about to fracture.
For him there was no love more crucial
than his love for this child, transcending creed
or doctrine, holding all our hope and history
in his arms. Your mother's hands were lovely, too,
and more than adequate to any task,
however modest she may have been, or shy.

Places We Could Never Find Alone

Valentine Luncheon, Santa Fe, 2008

The kind of beauty every man
Envies her husband for
Declares, just before her salad,
That she is anti-Valentine.

"One day a year he's expected
To be romantic, and
That's it? I don't think so." Across
The table another beautiful woman

Insists, "I'll take romance, any
Where, any time," and looks
Meaningfully at her husband.
In my own mind, two images appear:

Of walking into our bedroom
To find you standing by
The bed pushing a blue pillow
Into the side of your face.

"What are you doing?" "Testing it
For softness." Of course, I think,
How else? And then the other,
At my grandmother's farm

Soon after we were married, and
Years since I had last come here,
To this place that was for me
The still point at the center

Of the turning world. How that first
Morning I had gotten up at
Sunrise and walked around the pond,
Then turned back towards the house

To see you, in pajamas
And robe, barefoot, coming
To meet me through the wet grass:
How love brings us to those places
We could never find alone.

9

Christmas Eve

Do you remember the candlelight service
At St. Andrews, when Sabeth, kneeling, rested
Her forehead against the hard edge of the pew?
You thought something might be wrong, and asked
"Are you all right?" She was weeping. "It's so
beautiful," she said. And it was: the elemental
light, the acolytes in white like spirits
floating in the darkened church, the music,
a capella, transcending time and space,
creating a dimension of its own.
"I love it so much," she said, and we saw
her whole life, or the heart of it, and how
this moment held her, fragile and filled with joy.
I think we both prayed, silently, then,
Without confessing to each other,
I know I did, that in our life together
When faced by stress, or grief, or terrible loss
We find our way back here, to share again
This peace, this joy, this unconditional,
Complete, and all-encompassing love.

Directions

How to imagine yourself a bird: first
let every breath inflate balloons
inside your body. Let every breath
fill your bones with air.
Move most of your muscles to your chest.
Lean forward. Let your hips migrate
up backbone until your tilted body
balances. Move your big toe
to the back of your foot. Walk
on your toes. Replace your fingers
with strong primary feathers. Discard
the bones you do not need.
Cover your head and body and arms
with feathers, light and strong.
Shape the feathers on your arms to airfoils.
Hang your body in the air from outstretched
arms. Slide your shoulders
down your back until you balance.
Clap hands beneath your face. Feel
air twist the feathers at your wingtips.
Feel every feather at the tips of your wings
thrust you into air.
Feel air on your wings lift you up, hold you
firm. Construct a spacious curve
in the sustaining air.
Breathe. Fill your body with air. Fly.

How to imagine how I love you: first
imagine yourself a bird. Imagine
that bird to be me. Imagine that you
are air.

Snowstorm, St. Valentine's Day, 1990

Outside, it is snowing.
The air from edge to edge
Of our window is filled
With flying white points, graceful
Waves, undulating curves
Revealing the wind's shape,
Its shifting rise, swirl, and turn.

In the bare black tree taking
The window's center, one
Bright red cardinal, so
Tiny in that tree's complex
And tangled intersections
That at first I don't see him.

I don't know how long this
Red bird has been sitting
In the tree's storm-wracked heart,
Holding on against the wind
And snow. I do understand

That love, unexpected,
Is like this cardinal, and
Realizing that I love
you worked just like this.

How long had it been there
bright in the bare branches
of my life? Me, how blind?

Nocturne

Wind and shadow of night rise up together.
We have not finished working in the yard,
but we will go in for an evening meal,
a film, and then delicious sleep, your legs
beneath the comforter locked around mine like
the roots of two trees who have grown so close
underground I cannot tell which foot's mine,
which is yours. Tomorrow we will appear
as different to our friends as maple and
magnolia, as alike as shadow and wind.

There Ain't No Sanity Clause, but Love Doesn't Care

Whereas there is much that matters
and just as much that doesn't,
and whereas telling what does from
what doesn't is never easy,
the party of the first part (that
would be me) herewith promises
to do my dead-level, honest-
to-God best to discover,
acknowledge, and respect what
matters most to the party of
the second part (that would be you)
and when the aforesaid party
of the first part stacks his books in
huge piles on the floor instead
of on the shelves where they belong,
he will remove them within
a reasonable time as specified
by the party of the second
part, and furthermore when the party
of the second part cries and slams
down things in the kitchen and about
the house, the party of the first
part will understand that sometimes
disorder can overwhelm
and will reassure the party
of the second part that he
still loves her, and that things will
work out in time, and in time, with
patience and understanding,
all manner of things will be well.

I Can't Give You Anything But . . .

Come live with me and be my love
and we will all these pleasures prove:
first: to touch you with the small
tip of my tongue, lightly, at all

your corners where one deep bone
articulates against another bone.
Second: to let my fingers brush
like rollers and sweepers in a carwash

down your long clean back.
Third: to listen to the tack
and turn of your voice so closely
that I hear the start and close

of every phoneme. Fourth: to make you clothes
out of all my consonants. Fifth: to stay close
and still give you room. Sixth:
to arrange vowels for you and fix

them when they break. Seventh: to honor
your whims and doubts as if they were
my own, and everything you are afraid of,
if you will live with me and be my love.

Another Birthday

e la bellezza mia tutta ricerca in me
        —*La Bohème*, Act II

I remember that Brench called me, trying
To be tactful. We had just started dating.
"Saturday is her 50th birthday,
And we want to put on a little skit.
Would you be willing to play a small part,
Just for fun?" My role was to be a critic,
My only line, from time to time and with
Different inflections, "Tired, but promising."
Make it a question: "Tired?" "Promising?"
Or faint praise, almost an apology:
"Tired, BUT (pause for one beat) promising."
The trick was intonation, rise or fall
In the voice's pitch, and timing. The text
Was your career to date: attendant
To the Queen of the Night, tormenting
Papageno and Tamino, or
A lovesick boy in Faust. That role
Earned the critic's line your friends had
So much fun with. Your triumph was Musetta,
And everyone could see how beautiful,
Not tired, more than fulfilling your promise!
But then you had your family. A tight group:
The Bodens, Brewers, Regneris, and Clines.
One of them showed me a picture taken
Years after you sang Musetta. You might
Have been forty, riding a child's tricycle
In the driveway, leaning hard into a turn,
The tricycle tiny, your knees sticking out
Like huge wings. "We thought you ought to know,"
Barbara Brewer said, "what you're getting into."
Twenty-one years ago today.

Another Valentine (2009)

Language governs smugly,
so the studies tell us,
largely in our left
brain's domain (*sinister*,
Latin would have it) but
then while words wait to be
called on, some impatient—
It is St Valentine's
day—I'm listening to Brahms,
the violin concerto,
and I remember our nap
this afternoon, how your
body wrapped around me
and sleep came like falling
into the world's richest
treasure, and how, when my
father told me, "Son, you
will never be closer
to God than in the arms
of the woman you love,"
I thought he was talking
about sex, and only
now realize how sex
is more like the cocktail
before dinner, that makes
every taste closer than
thought, certainly closer
than languages, to those
essentials of being
alive that neither
words, nor music, nor lines
we have scraped onto paper
or stone can ever get
correct, entirely, but
when we, by whatever
mystery of human
love become part of,
we are in our whole selves,
left and right brain, body,
all we are together,
  bound, blessed beyond telling.

Anniversary, after the Grand Canyon, *et al*

Two weeks of rocks and canyons,
Famous, millions visiting,
And we come home to quiet,
A small round pond, centered
on a thin column of water
From an inexpensive pump
That keeps enough oxygen
In the water for our five
Shy fish. Water, gravity,
Wind, and more than a million
Years, indifferent to our
Need to understand, have bared
Earth's moods: wet, dry, wet, daring
Us to make sense of—which some,
Facing down the cost, attempt.

Eighteen years ago, only
Eighteen years, we vowed to share
What water, wind, gravity,
And time would do to us and
Those we love. Some have been hard.
Water cuts through stone. Wind carves.
Gravity and time, on their
Own inevitable scale,
Reshape us all. What does not
Change between us sanctifies
Our changing world, and our lives
Together, here, belonging.

Our Lives, Volcanic, Wait Our Waking

Bradley in the Room of Death

We know you well enough to imagine
What the séance was like: the believers
And those who really want to believe, all
Solemn, honoring every ritual—
The darkness, the solitary candle—
While you ask question after embarrassing
Question: "When do we get to see the ghost?
How do we know this ghost will tell the truth?
He never did when he was alive.
What's he going to do, move this water
Glass? He moved plenty of glasses in his
Lifetime, but not one with water in it."
The medium, challenged, has to defend
Herself: "You don't believe? Prove it then. Spend
One night here, alone, in the Room of Death."
"Sure," you say, cheerful as life itself.
The medium leads you into another
Room with walls as black as the first, with no
Windows, no furniture, and just the one
Door. "This is the true portal," she says,
"To the other world. No one has slept here
And lived." "Then I guess I'll have to stay
Awake, won't I?" you say. And to your friends
Gathered in candlelight outside the room,
"I'll see you in the morning, or if not,
I guess at the next séance." The medium
Shuts the door. In the plain light of morning
You come out grinning. "What's for breakfast?"
"How was it?" Someone asks. "Dark, very dark."
"Did you see anything?" "No, it was dark."
"Did you hear anything?" "Not a thing. No,
Wait, it does seem like I heard a faint voice,
Singing *Come Hither Love to Me*. It might
Have been my mother. But then again
I could have been dreaming. But wait, it's
Coming back to me now. It was Elvis."
And you sing to us in Elvis's rich voice,
"*I can't help falling in love with you.*
How does that start?" And thus, by seeming
To hold nothing sacred, you bring us face-
To-face with the world we live in, day by day.

Values of Fundamental Constants Adjusted
for John Reisert

*In the least-squares procedure, each input datum is weighted
according to the inverse square of the uncertainty of its value.
An additional complication is that bad data (measured values of
constants that differ from the "true" values by many times the
nominal uncertainties listed in the literature) must be eliminated.
Science, vol 235 (6 February 1987), p. 634.*

"I'll just finish up here and drive myself to the hospital."

There are some things that for now
seem never to change: atomic weights,
the speed of light in a vacuum, the rest mass
of an electron, positions of the fixed stars.

We believe this is not true and mistrust
our senses on purpose, building instead
a history in our minds of a time when time
was not time. We set about gathering

evidence, all of it circumstantial,
skeletons of energy, echoes of skeletons,
and shadows of the bones of light.
All the same we keep measuring,

knowing that we must trust and distrust
ourselves, that all the time
pieces of atoms whirl and spin
within us, through us, pieces of atoms

that began in the aneurysms of stars,
knowing that when we lie down
and count on the curling heat of our bodies
we can get no closer than the inverse square

of the uncertainty of its value, knowing
that when we wake up we must recalculate
and may have to live with many times
the nominal uncertainties listed in the literature.

Sam's Grandfather's Watch

Sam still owns the farm and, weekends,
goes out to check on things: his grandfather's
house has turned the color of cabbage. Hard
as turnips, the pasture rises in those

same three hummocks, still divided into
its own counties by dandelions, clover,
thistle and millet. Some things take a long time
to change. The tobacco field still produces

tobacco, though a neighbor works it now
for a percentage. When Sam was a boy
working that field in July, his grandfather
timed Sam's visits to the well, whipping out

his watch like an account book, snapping it
open, aiming it at him while the bucket
came up dripping, full of water, and heavy.
Sam told his grandmother, "When that old man

dies, I want his watch." And in time, it came
to him. He takes it with him every weekend,
sets it down on the stone wall around the well,
and walks the fields. He has never wound it up.

Funeral Stories

If you do not have at least one story
to tell, what do you do after the funeral?
Best perhaps if you have a story you
probably shouldn't tell. "Preacher," he said,
when he woke up in the hospital,
"if I'd had one more drink I'd have caught
that goddam car." That kind of story.

Deep Spring in Florida
for Bill and Joy Hunt

Somewhere in central Florida there is
a spring that no one has found the bottom
of. Friends who live near this spring take us there
and tell us some of the stories—divers
trapped under rocks so deep they lost all
sense of up and down, swimming deeper to
find fresh air and waiting friends. Can it really
be all that deep? Just look. And we stare down
through water so clear it disappears, down
beyond a huge projecting rock into
accumulating darkness, down to where
we can only imagine seeing.
Who would want to go down there? We all do,
my friend says. Some go. Some of us just want to.

Visiting Poet at Shakertown

Our guide through these quiet buildings
was short and hefty—nobody's
centerfold—but you saw
some tiny curl in her smile,
a twist towards self-indulgence
like a cat's delight in sunlight,
a mind that recognized pleasure
the way yours did
(No machine can measure
how you love women!)
and so, for the rest of the tour—

But actually before we found her,
even before we'd walked through
the stone gate into the well-cropped
village, fields and buildings
in calm array, you were asking
"Did they really not? They must
have." From the start you looked
for places they might have slipped
away to, a man and a woman together.

The guide's description of their worship,
men and women safe on separate sides
of the simple hall, dancing and shaking,
didn't stop you from looking
into corners and closets. And when
she showed us the upstairs, modern
hotel rooms with solid hotel
bathrooms, white and clean, you
stayed behind, and she, and the door
blew shut, only long enough
for you to come out grinning, your
plans made, and then we walked outside,
into the fields as wide and bright
and cared for as only those places
we count on to save us can be.

Picasso's Late Drawings
for John Guenther

Sometimes this is what happens
When an artist gets old: obsessed
With sex, he abandons all modesty.

The bodies of women enlarge and flatten,
Become all lines and twists and spaces.
He begins to make the familiar faces

Of old friends look like cavalier
Lovers, figures from his memory
That energetic spiraling lines invest

With the energy they bragged about
When they were young, wanting to do what
Now he only draws, again and again. Bodies

Are represented by their most important parts.
Old jokes rise up. He actually starts
Drawing breasts like melons. Nudes stare

Wantonly at the artist, who exposes
What they hid and he spent a lifetime looking
For. At this age he feels free to worship

Flesh, and not inclined to color in their hearts.

Ohio Flood

for Aleda Shirley

If the light startled the sleeping lovers,
imagine what the crew of the towboat
thought: houses rising from the river
and, behind the windows of one, ignited
in the brilliant spot of light,
the naked skin of a man and woman,
their arms, throats, and shoulders the color
of buttermilk. The helmsman swings the light
downstream, leaving them to each other,
and in the wide wet darkness
fights the current to line up
with the McAlpine Locks. He reads the markers,
red right returning, and considers
that they really were naked, and did,
in his brief groping light, turn towards
each other, devil take the high water,
and then lie down, to wrap like weeds
around each other through the night.

Epithalamion
for Brittany and Scott

To know another's mind
Almost better than you
Know your own—to taste her
Joy by how her eyebrows
Bow towards you, her grief
By how her tight shoulders
Hold themselves as still as
Death, and know that loving
Her beyond the death you
Know is coming cannot
Cushion grief, or make it
Go away. But you are
There, and know that she knows
Her grief belongs to you
As well, and all the joys
You bring each other now.

Early morning, Maui, looking west by south

Clouds lie over Lanai like a lover
Or like the island's spirit shape, lifted
During the night into the air, the same curve
That rises from the sea rising as bright
Sunlit cloud, while ocean at the island's
Foot, still shadowed from the rising sun by
Maui's western mountains, waits for light.
All calm the day begins. Early walkers
Breathe in the energy that waits, inhaling
The day's balance. Heat and gravity and wind
Will shape the ocean. Deep flowing currents
We cannot see shape the land we live on.
Our lives, volcanic, wait our waking.
Grace and beauty ours for the taking.

Cocktails, Early Evening

Here on the southwest side of Maui, high
Above the surf's incessant sighing, these
Two couples celebrate retirement.
They sit down for cocktails on the windy
Deck of their condominium. They talk
About their lives, their families, their troubled
Children, one in jail, one deeply depressed,
Both determined to do nothing to help
Themselves, or so it seems. Memory
Proves a fickle witness: they cannot agree
On who said what, or when, or how it hurt.
They do agree that love is hard, much harder
Than they dreamed when they married, so many
Years ago, before these tears, this quiet joy.

Artificial Insemination Clinic

Stacks of *Playboys*, as if at twenty-three
you didn't have imagination enough.
Now you speak of all those children you might
have, children in their forties, forever
unaware of where the color of their
eyes or hair came from, their skill at telling
jokes, their tendencies towards skepticism,
their love of argument and turn of phrase.

But in particular you talk about
that one time you opened the wrong door
and saw, before a nurse who looked like your
mother closed the door in your face, saw,
you said, a thin young woman on a cold
table, knees up, frightened. Could you have loved her?

A Suicide

1.

At first we knew only that something
terrible had happened, and then who
held its center, like the hurricane's
still eye, but still not certain how
(or how terribly true) that image
had already become, and then word
that his funeral was scheduled, that
he may have shot himself, that he did it
at his favorite spot on the farm,
a green meadow beside the thick woods
where there was a spring, and a view downhill
to the lake. Where his wife found his body.
Something about money, a tax audit,
his bookkeeping. We did not believe it.

2.

He was practical, funny at parties,
good at almost everything he did.
He went to work for his dad, even though
the old man was a tyrant, and he stayed,
cheerfully, in the face of his father's
daily condemnations. He married
and raised decent kids, remembering
every time they fell short how his father
told him what he couldn't do, never
be capable of, often with his friends
waiting, hovering like frightened fish
at the bottom of the yard. He told
his own there was nothing they couldn't do,
nothing, if they wanted to bad enough.

3.

At his funeral we remember
the parties, his laugh you could recognize
from outside the house, and how, if we asked,
he'd help with anything, as if he knew

every skill you needed to build a house
or rebuild it, how he never insisted
but you knew he was right. In the narthex
where his coffin waited for the procession,
each one of us, in secret, touched it,
wanting to say, You didn't have to do
this, not knowing all the circumstances
but certain nothing, not sin nor shame
nor father's curse, could cost a man this much.
Wanting to say that, having lost the chance to.

Your First Lover

I think of him with his wife
and his daughter. Did his memory
of you ever come between his married eye
and brain? Did his knowledge
of your body twisted naked
backwards while you waited
for him to make up his mind
ever tighten his hips against
his wife's lovely hips?
Did she smile at him then?

Did he watch his daughter
and think of your tight legs, cold
under the covers, while guilt
ignited like indigestion, until
he told you to get dressed? Did he
think, seeing his child in a child's dresses,
of you poised over him in his front seat?
Did he finally feel murder take
your father's shape inside himself?

My tongue, waiting for your tongue

My tongue, waiting for your tongue
tries out a small lie,
safe in its solitude, aware
of the importance of practice. While

your tongue is still missing,
my tongue plays with other
languages: the curl
of a German adjective: *schön*,

a phrase in slide-and-touch
French: *je t'aime.*
My tongue waiting for your tongue
touches the backs of my own

teeth, considers the taste
of darkness, hungers
after your bitter dark places
where it can never reach far

enough. My tongue, waiting
for your tongue, true
or false, lies dumb,
lies shapeless, lies alone.

Been There, Done That

Let me tell you how you go
through detox when your drug of
choice is another person
who does not choose you under
any circumstances. First,
remember that this is like
instrument flying: take your
eyes off the gauges and you're
a goner. Second, what feels
right almost certainly is
not what it feels like, and what
feels wrong is probably right.
She is both bad weather and
the hard rocks that hide in it.
Get on the radio. Trust
Air Traffic Control. Do not
fly by the seat of your pants.

A 50th Wedding Anniversary

As fishes move in water, birds in air,
We take on time when we marry,
And move in time like golden fish, or flocks
Of birds, no single fish or bird aware
Of who decides, who leads, or where
Their turning will take them. Rising together
Or descending, we move with grace, gravity
Itself undone by time's sustaining dare,
And our determined willingness to care.

Terra Incognita

Prairie Lighthouse

For the little girl who was born outside
of Strasburg, North Dakota, whose father
read to her, throughout the long winter,
stories in Dutch—her favorite about
another little girl whose father kept
a lighthouse, who lived in Holland with tides
and seabirds, sailboats and barges.

In the North Dakota winters, this child
went to the bathroom in the boarded walkway
between the house and barn: it was too cold
outside even for her father, who had shoes.

In fifty years, she never left Strasburg.
She raised twelve children. She saw no more
of the ocean than the slow rise and fall
of prairie under the moon. She never knew
that killdeer from the summer pastures raced
in winter ahead of wave after wave
on the sand of Atlantic beaches. And she
never forgot the idea of those sailboats
in the sea air, or the sweeping oars of light.

Dragon

He has huge lungs. He inhales
for twenty minutes or more.
Right before he exhales, we hear
his air ignite with a breathy thump.

Frederick says it's just the furnace,
but we know his ancient lineage:
worm and fire, the anger
of guarding your own treasure,
keeping precious metal warm
and comfortable to touch.

Every night through the winter
we sleep snug as gold.

Jean Louise at the Ninth Grade Prom

The dress my father bought me:
an elaborate skeleton, a thousand

tiny white bones,
a delicate, balanced scaffold,

a fog over gravel,
an open cage.

Going Off the Air

Our children don't know what that means.
Cable TV is never not there.
Satellite radio? Around the clock.
But stations used to shut down at midnight
or maybe One A.M. Trust me.
After the last symphony, a brief
gesture to tomorrow's weather
which no one entirely believed,
and then the station's four letters: a word,
an acronym, or random letters,
always beginning with W.
Then they played something emotional
or patriotic: "The Star Spangled
Banner" or "My Old Kentucky Home,"
something like that. And then with no
other sign or warning, except
perhaps the promise of a Six
A.M. resurrection, they shut
down, quit broadcasting, went off
the air. If you left your radio on
you heard this hissing sound, which now
they tell us is the sound of the beginning
of the universe. Believe me. It did happen.

Sex Education

We cannot escape living with lunatics,
Sometimes becoming the lunatics we live with,
Terrified to confront the energy,
The earth-spinning energy that hums, deep
Down, and drives our hidden lives, most terrified
It will destroy our children, if they find out.

But She's Not You

She's everything a man could want . . .
—E. Presley

For three years I've tried to build a woman
to take your place. Right now she looks
pretty good, considering.

I'd hoped to find her with all the good parts
pre-assembled, ready to roll. Nothing
comes to us perfect.

I've been fooled by flesh-and-blood synecdoche
more than once: a waitress because her bones
were crisp as celery, a dancer

whose tight hair caught and held like velcro
against the fabric of my skin, a French teacher
for her tongue's rasp and turn

in my mouth. I've got her almost done.
She's everything I ever wanted, somewhat
pieced together. I'll be finished

when I find what's left that only you have:
the way you see around the sharp corners
of what I say, what I think, and what I want.

Until I find that,
she is not you and will not do.

A Country Life

How he was born to farm, still
A child when he directed
His first plow, leaning left, then
Right, holding on for dear life,
Shouting *Gee* and *Haw*, while his
Father watched, knowing the mule
Knew the field and understood
With mule sense more than the child.
How all his life he would farm,
Owning the place after his
Father, long beyond having
To wrestle the plow, or talk
To mules. Forty years later,
The young people, his nephews
And nieces, looked at him
As if they were visiting
A museum. He never
Missed church: weddings, funerals,
Burying one brother, one
Sister-in-law, one nephew
Who died young. Now his family
Has gathered together here,
Wishing, praying, for this good
Man, grace, peace in his going.

Nutt Cracks Up

Baptist preacher and television humorist Grady Nutt died
last night when the twin-engine chartered plane he was
returning home in crashed just after takeoff.

In the single heartbeat between
settling into the dark trip home
and the certainty of the hard field
opening like a handslap
out of the rain
Grady probably told a joke—
Did you hear the one about—
and went laughing into the ground,
while the pilot stood on the rudder
and the copilot checked the fuel switches
until physics sucked all their time
through the smashing windshield.

When air failed, he would lift them,
laughing, out of themselves.
The rest of us can only follow, listening
to the echo of laughter, like the ring
of the sanctuary after a hymn,
just before the prayer. Did we listen
close enough to hear what sang
in every punch line, every
pun? A thousand tongues of praise.

Queen of Cats, in Purple Raiment
for Teresa

You do not own the patent on suffering
Or on strange behavior, though you may at
One time have applied for both. A few of us
Remember when you sought love voraciously
And clawed your way out of every corner
Love backed you into. Fertile as every
Feral stray you took in, birth threatened you
Year after desperate year. Following your
Only child, you stretched into loveliness.
When you adopted a color, we thought
The color of sunset just before dark
Suits. It's the color of communion wine.
The color stayed. So did the cats. And your son.

Map Fragment, on Clay

Who first thought of scratching *here* and *there*
on soft clay, instead of only giving
directions, must have wanted to keep close
the shape of all that lay between himself
and someone whose absence turned regular days
and nights into a vast *terra incognita*, a blank
that his mind filled with terrifying beasts, winged
serpents, who sang of other courses, other
islands, other ways. If he drew the place
he knew, and those distant places he thought
he knew, he could touch the map where she was
and say to himself, without leaving home,
if she is not here, she is there.

Purple Martins in a Rainshower

After three days of record-setting heat
a late afternoon thunderstorm builds itself
west of the river, changing the sky's color
from shimmering blue to the gray and black of concrete

strewn with ashes, heavy with charcoal and shadows.
Small thunder introduces, like clearing a throat,
drops of rain, at first timid, then
steady, their voices the shuffling of many pages.

Suddenly the air above the yard is filled
with purple martins, flying in quick arcs
around each other as if they were weaving
rain into cool and invisible sheets.

What are they really doing, these flyers
who rarely land, who eat and drink in the air,
who nest, like all lovers, high above everything
firm, who to fly look down and let go?

Ferris Wheel

Riding the antipodes of the Ferris Wheel,
while he and I are rising
to level with a fugitive balloon
and intercept the last dark solitary swift
and discover Clark's old bridge against the night,
you and she descend
towards the whirling enterprise of lights
and children screaming. As you two are lifted
out of the screaming children, towards the silent moon,
a colder, darker sky, a lost bird flying,
we two fall towards the screams and lights.

Through the turning hub, the steel
that holds us holds you at its other end.
Lifted, falling, we around each other wheel.

Driving to Work

Birds stand in the middle of the road
early in the morning, starlings and robins,
while around them, above the lawns,
the fields, the fairways and greens of the park,
mist gives visible presence to the air.

There is nothing to eat in the road,
and cars (like mine now passing
the park entrance) charge down on them,
as if getting to work were the most
important thing on the face of the warming earth.

At the last minute, they fly up. They think
with their eyes, and save themselves. We
pay more attention to the clock on the dash
and traffic reports on the radio. Had they larger
brains, they might marvel at our clumsiness.

Scientists Coat Termites with Slow-Acting Poison

From the *New York Times*:
"Social by nature, the termites
lick each other, spreading
the poison." It makes you think
about the word *social*,
doesn't it? As in
ice cream social, or
today Miss Universe
attended a social gathering,
or Church social next
Sunday. Bring your own
slow-acting poisons.
Make sure they are sweet.

Bifocals

It would never happen to me, that,
once I put on glasses, I would need more, that
I would be so old I would ever need
not one lens but two, stacked before
my eyes, like air over water.

There I was, not all bird or fish,
looking at her hair, searching her eyes,
now small or large as I bob my head up
and down, trying to decide which vision
shows her to me truer, deep down.

Cheat light and time, of course, is what
bifocals do: stack lenses up, air and water.
My eyes dive down when I read her skin,
fly up when there is distance between us.
Let light be steady and time change,

as they will: my bifocals bend them both,
using their stubborn sameness to see her better,
near or far, until my eyes have had
enough of time, and light: never enough
to see, near or far, enough of her.

Family Suidae, Genus Sus, Species domestica

Despite their reputation for gluttony, [pigs] are generally social and intelligent animals.
(Wikipedia)

Pigs in the Sun

Flank against flank, they press
thigh and haunch and long side:
he feels her shape displace
his own. She yields, as always,

to his lean and bulge. Around them
flowers thrive, who learned long
ago to raise their heads above
the bend of stems pressed

by lolling pigs. The mud
bakes: a crisp chocolate patina
on pigs and stringy stems.
Exhale. Satisfied there is nothing

more to do, nothing more
perfect than pigs, pleased
with themselves, pleased to be
in love, pleased most of all

with the hot, hale, healing sun.

Feeding Pigs

The farmer calls, "Sooeey! Pig,
pig, pig, pig, pig!"
Flattered that he names them,
the pigs come running.

Their ears jiggle like turn signals.
They want to go both ways
at once. The warm slops
splash into their solid oak trough

polished by the forefeet
of generations who shouldered
to the front, who stood
balancing on the slippery steep

trough sides to suck down
the ripest dinner: half
a tomato, grapefruit rinds,
scrap of bacon, thin-sliced

and chewy, soaking in a warm broth
of sweet and sour milk.

The Smell of Pigs

The green mud, kneaded
into ripe, deep footprints,
the slops sour enough
to take rust off a shovel,

the fecal corner, the dusty
boards of the squat lean-to:
everything perfumes the pigs' home.
O reassuring familiarity!

While the pigs enjoy
their excellent dinner, the farmer
with his empty slopbucket
farts into the still air

and stands in his own
warm and pungent envelope.
The pigs understand, and eat
in secret thanksgiving

that he hides them here for himself
far from the white farmhouse,
farther even than the horse, and the cows.

Pigs in Cold Weather

When the mud freezes,
the pigs lie close
on the hard floor
of their low log hut

and listen for the call
to dinner. Every year
in this weather, one
pig leaves in the farmer's

big pickup truck.
Later, from a distance
almost mythical, a freezing
shriek slices through their huddle,

a squeal as boundless and sharp
as the double-pointed
beer bottles broken just beyond
the pen wire.

The pigs at home struggle
to their feet, snort
and fret, for no good reason
they can think of.

Carolina Gospel Old-Time Revival Week

for Page

Sunday Night: The Youth Fellowship

The heat in the church waits
as still as I thought prayer
should be: I count the hymns left
to sing. When the music starts,
a breeze sneaks through the open
double doors at the back
of the church and washes me
clean in the blood of July.
Outside, tree frogs sing their own
hymns, ignorant of the sweat
that beads in the wet bight
between the shoulder blades
of Jeanette Morgan, singing
two pews in front of me,
half a light year away.

Monday Night: The Preacher

For a month these services have hung
from every telephone pole between Raeford
and Pinehurst, with my name in huge letters
and my picture looking as if God

stood inside my skull, counting
the house. Lord, I am not
certain, and my father's world
has turned and turned on me.

When I was a child, we sang
on the lawn for a blessing, drank
bitter iced tea, ate country ham
and chocolate pie before we went

inside to listen to my father.
He tried to tell us that, if
we turned loose of ourselves, we'd
fall into a deep well, a well

that each self was only the rim
of, and at the bottom we'd find
ourselves as new as when we
step, steaming and soapy, from a tub

of scalding water. I knew
he would not lie to me and turned
loose, and I am still falling.
Perhaps I could not, even then,

let go the rim, and all my life
have only dreamed of falling.

Tuesday Night: The Old Folks

Rain in the early evening
works like a sharp knife
that releases the odors—
still warm from the garden—
of fresh tomatoes, cucumbers,
cabbages, and snapped green beans.

The heavy air inside the church dissolves
in the smell of dirt and cut grass,
pine needles, old leaves, and ozone.
The white shirts of the farmers dry
tight around their throats.
I draw in my very first
breath, every time I breathe.

We sing louder in the rain's
steady applause. If the air
always smelled like this, we might
be able to breathe forever.

Wednesday Night: Newlyweds

Halfway through the week, my life
balanced unshakably,
I consider not going
but do go, finally,
for Carolyn, who offers
me a bargain, and sweats
beside me in the hot air
while the preacher goes on and on.

I begin to wonder what sharp tool
the carpenter used, a hundred
and twelve years ago, to cut
these unforgiving pews.

At the door I say, "We almost
didn't come tonight." The preacher
shakes my hand like a lifeguard.
"What made you change your mind?
Not last night's sermon?" No.
It was sweet Carolyn, who
wants us both to be perfect
in attendance, just for
the idea of it, and who
promised we'd go to the lake,
afterwards, where the grass
is cut to the water's edge,
put down her mother's old quilt,
and swim naked. I can't tell him that.

Thursday Night: The Children

Inside is boring and the seats so hard
the two sides of your bottom start

to itch, to burn, to buzz numb.
In the heat I lay me down, head first,

in my mother's musty cotton lap,
and don't wake up until my father

settles me in my own cool bed.
By tomorrow I'll be ready to come back

because before the service Mike
and me and Kelly and Jake and Charlie

will chase the outlaw girls outside around
the church a dozen times, dodging old man

Perkins, who looks angry, and scowls
at every pass but forbids us not

and, with the first voice of a hymn,
leads us out of dusk into the bright

heat, itching, stillness, parents,
prayer, singing, and sleep.

Friday Night: The Mothers

For one meal, four hymns, two
prayers, and a sermon, I can forget
potato skins, dust behind the couch,
and underwear stuck to damp towels.

From inside the church I can hear
Jake and Charlie racing the others
around the building, can hear Mike
yell when his speed slings him
through the first row of headstones.
I stop my breath until he's free.

There are only women here. We are
centers, separate and alone, waiting
for the music to start, waiting
for the men who stand in a herd
outside the front door to join us.

We sip the quietness like hot coffee
after a meal and before the dishes.
Polly McGuire, who cannot sit
between all four children
at the same time, believes that here
even she can sing in tune.

Saturday Night: The Dead

I cannot tell the shouts of children
from the hymns of the adults. Voices
hum like a dream through the clay.

We have not missed a single service.
We were married here and lived
down the hill. By the time she died,
laws or some persuasive salesman
put her in a concrete vault
beside the earth I had become.

Listen. The service is over.
They are singing the final hymn.
Now two people walk together
above us. They kneel or lie down
under the tall tulip poplar.

Tomorrow we return to the usual
Sunday morning, the men outside
intent on testing their neighbors'
husbandry, their wives hiding
inside the dark church, their children
running through this cemetery, wild to grow.

Taking On Knowledge

Sands of Iwo Jima

Coincidence, two or more accidents our mind
connects by finding unconnected similar
details, becomes in film and fiction *irony:*

John Wayne, Sergeant Stryker, before they raise the flag
on Suribachi, saying "I never felt so
good in my life," and then the bullet hits.

I was ten when I saw the film, Carolina
Theater, Durham, NC, 1950:
a newsreel and a cartoon (*Bugs Bunny Nips the Nips*).

After the movie, we left, my father and I,
through the smell of popcorn in the lobby, where we found
ourselves beside a man who limped and used a cane.

"Good picture," my father said. "Not bad," the man said,
"Didn't come close to the real thing." "You were there?
What do you remember?" "How scared I was, getting

shot at, and no cover, no place to hide, couldn't
even dig a foxhole in that stuff. It wasn't
sand, it was ashes. Never saw a Jap until

after we'd taken Suribachi. They all stayed
underground. There were two flags, you know: little flag
and then a flag big enough to see from the other

end of the island. And the dead bodies. We lost,
we lost . . . ." He turned his face, and I thought he might weep.
"They killed John Wayne," I said. "They killed the Ringo

Kid." I was trying to be funny. To me
it was just a movie. "Our company, when
we hit the beach, over three hundred. Less than

a month, no more than fifty." He stabbed with his thumb
towards the dark screen. "They can't make a movie as
terrible as war." And then he turned away.

Courtly Love

"Wit ye well," said the queen, "I would
as fain as ye that ye might come in to me."
—Malory, *Le Morte d'Arthur*

Picture Guinevere inside a darkened room,
gazing through stone and iron at the rising moon.
Her wounded knights sleep in the room's recesses,
where she can treat their wounds with soft compresses,
salves, and ointments. They defended her honor
when her violent host forced himself upon her.
Her hand rests on the smooth, chilled wall.
She hears a noise outside the window: tall
Lancelot is there, climbing a shaky ladder.
If it weren't for the iron bars, he'd have had her.
Her breath comes through the bars, a hot whisper
touching him with slippery promises. He kisses her,
and, reaching with her tongue, she kisses him back,
safe behind bars, still faithful, and intact.
When Lancelot wrenches the bars away like toys,
what can she say? She whispers, "Make no noise,"
and leads the way. Her knights sleep on bricks
while, silent and intense, she teaches him tricks
he hasn't dared imagine. But it doesn't feel right,
this quiet, contrived jousting through the night.
Breaking in, he gashed his hand to bone.
Her silent twisting is not enough, alone,
to justify the bloody sheets, or crumbling stone.

Lavoisier's Diamond

It could sow light like seeds
in the cultivated eyes of the city.
On a long finger, it pointed;
on a fat one it seemed to whirl.
Lavoisier put one in a bottle
with a flame, until the diamond
caught fire and disappeared
in a breath of carbon dioxide.

That it burned at all amazed
many. That the weight
of carbon in the CO_2
equaled exactly the weight
of the diamond seemed frivolous
and wasteful: they missing
the point, that we too
being largely carbon
will weigh out just as true.

Hunting Frogs

When I was in the seventh grade,
a girl and I actually went, after school,
into the woods and believed
we were hunting frogs for the biology class,
even though it was October
and all the frogs had been asleep
for weeks in mud so deep
even the tremble
our footsteps made in the brittle leaves
never reached them. We planned it
days ahead. She brought bluejeans
and changed in the girls' restroom.
We found a fallen tree, just deep
enough in to hide us from the road,
and balanced on it. I cannot remember
when I admitted to myself I didn't
care about the frogs,
but, after I came home late, my pants
and shirt peppered with bark
and pieces of broken leaves, my father
never missed a chance to ask,
"Seen any frogs?" or if I were sulky,
"A wild frog hunt might cheer you up."

The Life Line
Winslow Homer (1884)

The deep hollow of the sea between
The rising face of one and frothing surf
Behind another wave: suspended over it
A woman, injured or unconscious, wet,
Cold, and hanging limp against the life ring
Of a breeches buoy, held there by this man
Whose face we cannot see, the shore-side
Whip line taut, pulling them towards safety.
Behind them gale winds tear away the sails
Of a foundering ship. The shore: a tall cliff,
And the spray of huge waves. He will hold her
Until they are safe, or both of them lost.
What kind of man will hazard his own life
In such a sea to save a shipwrecked stranger?

The Numbering at Bethlehem
Pieter Brueghel, the Elder (1566)

Somewhere in this crowd, there is
A man leading a donkey,
And his wife, pregnant with her
First child, is riding. They need
To find a place to stay. This
Town is not their home, though he
May have come as a child to
Visit family. They have
No friends here, and now her time
May be close. Neither of them
Has done this before. Neither
Knows what to expect. No one
In the crowd has time to help.
Will this night change anything?

Snap the Whip
Winslow Homer (1872)

You know the game: everybody
runs hard as they can, holding hands,
and then the boy on the near end
suddenly stops, sets his feet hard
against the ground, and the others
swing, like a gate made of children,
swinging faster the farther out,
fighting centrifugal force now
to keep from being flung away,
flung out of the sudden circle
this line of children has become
a radius of, and those farthest
out have to hang on for dear life.
What saves them is how tight they and
their friends can hold on, and for how
long. Those farthest from the center
need the strongest friends.

Siren

When Odysseus tied himself to the mast,
did he know that taking on
knowledge was as dangerous as taking
on water? Was he, father-like,

caring for his sailors, to protect
them from something worse than sinking?
Or did he care only for his own
huge cleverness and the need of cleverness

to put his body in the way
of knowledge? Think about the sailors,
rowing through numb silence, after
years of the ocean wind's whip and shout:

how much his cleverness depended
on their faithful lack of curiosity. But
then look at Odysseus: skillfully roped,
carried hard into the fresh breeze of your

innovative voice. Look at Odysseus,
helpless and deliberate: how could you,
from your sharp submerged rocks, fail
to love him? How could you not

sing for him higher and lower
than for any fool who'd tack toward you
at your first arpeggio? And how could he
not love you for promising him

a new course to knowledge? But the rocks,
the rocks that harbor you are hard to see,
under the waves that rise and swirl, pull and spin,
and getting out is as dangerous as getting in.

A ReDeDeconstructionist translates the Odyssey

Of course I don't read Greek. Why should that make
any difference since the text is, you know,
unreliable? What I make of it
isn't up to you or anybody else.
Besides, I've read a dozen boring versions.
If the poem had been written recently
here in the U. S. of A., or better
yet in France, it would go like this, except
I don't read French either, so think of this
as a translation of French from the Greek
as it would be if I could read either
language. What I'm fluent in, well, you could
call it "literature." Here we go:

Use me, Muse, to tell the story of that
slick, tricky hero who got lost time
after time, trying to get home from Troy.
Tell how he, most persuasive of captains
could not persuade his own crew to puleez
leave the cattle of the sun god alone.

Start where he's held captive, yeah, by that
cute immortal piece, that gorgeous nympho
(nymph, I meant to say) Kalypso, after
all the others had got home, long after,
so long after that Athena herself
goes to Zeus, picking her time carefully,
while Poseidon, the one god still pissed off
at Odysseus (who had, after all,
blinded Poseidon's son and bragged about
it), while Poseidon is out of town.

Athena catches Zeus in the middle
of this long complaint about humanity,
specifically Orestes killing
Aigisthos who'd killed Agamemnon whose
wife he'd been, well, friendly with, the whole time
Agamemnon was away (she still pissed
at Ag since he clearly thought this stupid
war was more important than his family,

in particular his daughter, and then
Agamemnon brought a whole crowd home, in-
cluding this slave girl who he himself was—
I don't think I have to spell it out) and
Hermes had warned Aigisthos, Don't do this.
But men, when it comes to women, are just
not rational.

        I've got to stop here for
the time being: there's this committee thing,
a colleague at the University
thinks requiring students to read Shakespeare
is too old fashioned, and besides she knows
why Goneril and Regan turned on Lear,
a clear case of sexual abuse when
they were just girls (the bastard got what he
deserved). There's going to be a vote, so
I have to be there. I'll finish this anon.

Teaching Blind

Her voice held our attention as it did
forty years of students: "He was the worst
student I ever had. We saved his projects
to show all the others what not to do.

Goes without saying, he failed. Next semester,
he shows up in my class again. Half way
through the semester he's got an F, so
he stands up and says *I've taken this class*

*a semester and a half and you ain't
taught me nothin!* No, I said, I can't
teach you anything. Matter of fact,
I can't teach anybody anything.

But **you** can **learn**. He looked like I had hit
him in the face. End of the semester
he had a B. And graduated.
And became a teacher. Heartbreaking

thing, I saw in the paper, about ten
years later, he'd dropped dead during recess
of a heart attack. Kids' favorite
fifth grade teacher." There were tears pooling

in her eyes as she told us. Funny, how
love can lie in wait, sometimes for years,
how it can shape our thinking, all we do,
without our knowing, or that we might want it to.

First Words
for Flora Naslund

Now is the only time in all
your life that language will do
exactly what you want it to.

Say *bird*, and the bright paper shapes
overhead spring into flight. Other flying
things have the same name, and sing.

Some words are hard to pronounce
right now, but you wrinkle your nose
and concentrate on those

difficult positions for your lips and tongue:
out comes *owl*, and someone around you
hoo-hoots, hoo-hoots, on cue.

Make the sound yourself, and someone
will say *owl*. Enjoy it while
it lasts: language will soon enough smile,

deny, make up stories.
Now you can say, when your mother asserts
herself, *I know*, and these two words

delight her as much as it will take
a novel to, when you are grown.
At the bottom of the stairs, alone,

you say, *I made it*, and your father
acts as if you meant an epic.
A sentence is like a magic trick:

you begin with red and blue silks
and end up with an exotic
red, white, and blue rabbit.

But words right now are beams of light
that touch the world's seventy times seven
wonders for you. It must be heaven

to find for the first time that the stone
satyr in the yard, where all the sticks
are, has *your nose*, and that on those *red bricks*

he waits patiently, day after wordless
day, for you to say your name.
Flora Kathryn, the world will never be the same

now that you have words in your pretty *noggin*.

Learning To Swear

A mother of three asked herself, Where, oh
where do children learn these words? And when? Who
would know better than their teachers, she thought,
and devised a questionaire. She sent it
to every teacher in the county, first
through eighth grades: Please check the box beside
the words you hear your students use. Feel free to
add comments, or any words I have not
thought of, on the back of this paper.
For purposes of this study only
indicate the grade you teach. Your response
will be kept in strictest confidence. Then,
the words (a list). Every teacher answered.
Their data suggested a learning curve.
First the fun of using words you were not
supposed to even know. Then, very soon
after, that words can hurt if hurled against
another, and any noun or verb become
a name. Last, the safety valve, that all
these words turned loose in anger or frustration,
one at a time, or several in a grand
accumulation, can cure the hurt, if
only for a brief and fragile spell.

Open Enrollment, a Lament

Every semester, these students show up:
they think commas create dramatic,
pauses, they spell by ear, they confuse
idea with **ideal**, they get frantic

before tests, they seem to care
about their grades far more than what
is there to discover. Even the air
seems to threaten them with failing.

The faculty don't deserve them, clearly.
The faculty have their doctorates. They could be
teaching somewhere more important, where
graduate scholars could appreciate their skills

at generating frequent publications
from almost nothing, in several languages,
on soft money. Meanwhile, they deconstruct
these: ignorant, hopeful, helpless, dangling.

Invocation for an Acceptance to Graduate School
for Bernie Carducci

All praise and thanksgiving to almighty God,
creator of the heavens and the earth
and of all who live thereon,
and special praise and thanksgiving
for the creation of human beings,
and academic communities, faculty,
staff, and administrators, and for those
who teach, and those who learn, and those
who would take us by the hand to help us
do both better. We ask your forgiveness
for those hurtful things we have done to one another,
or not done to one another when we should have,
and especially your forgiveness for the formation
of academic and administrative committees
which have wasted everyone's time
and brought great bitterness among us
and subjected us to University Politics
and meetings beyond number. But chiefly
we come before you today to ask
your blessing on this child, Rozana Carducci,
who, because of her father's wisdom and experience,
should know better but has decided anyway—
led no doubt by your greater wisdom
and purpose—to earn an advanced degree
and to toil among the academics. Guard her
from jealousy, envy, backbiting, gossip,
complaints to the dean, and all other snares
and traps that academics set for each other.
Guide her into the paths of graciousness
and generosity that cross every campus,
no matter how cleverly we have hidden them.
Bless her in her work and in her play,
and grant that all of us gathered here
receive such grants, sabbaticals, raises,
and promotions as we are needful of
to do your work and to build an impressive
retirement portfolio. All of this we ask
in the name of him whose teaching evaluations
were excellent, but who did not publish,

and who went to Glory at your right hand
untenured, except in your grace
and love everlasting. Amen.

Introduction to Creative Writing

My students are making lists of words:
powerful verbs and interesting nouns.
Then they have to switch, select

interesting verbs and powerful nouns.
Words rise up out of their murmur:
eruption, stench "We have that one,"

somebody from a rival group
calls out. The first group answers,
"But you don't have *body odor*."

Brainstorm is what they are doing,
and they begin to discover how words,
like two-way mirrors, show them

an unguarded world, some things
they only see from their side. From
the back of the room, laughter.

Aphrodisiac hovers over their heads.
(Are they still into interesting,
or have they moved on to powerful?)

One group discovers derivations:
voltage, intercommunication. Another
group finds simple words: *wish,*

hit, score. One group, entirely
young women, sits quietly, almost
whispering: *hope, love, care.*

Sleeping with Bees

They swarm around me, a restless blanket,
warm with the rasp of brittle wings.
They have promised not to sting me, and I trust
that even a lone worker, crushed

by, say, my shoulder when I roll over,
will keep the hive's faith, suck in
the needle and venom at his abdomen's end
and die *pro patria*. Why

have they asked me to sleep here? Because
when I doze off, they plan to send
an elite team, skilled at finding
lost flowers, into the petals of my ears,

deep into my sinuses, to find
the pollen of words. *"We can only
speak of sun and blossoms, bearings
and ranges. Teach us to say*

NOT, or IF." I dream I am flying.
Sunlight bisects my eye and wing.
I am flying towards a color
field-wide, filled with pollen,

flexing under the wind in long
waves. That color has no name.

Yellow Bird
for Bonnie Kendall

On the porch of the trading post, an old
man, an Indian, asked her, "You a teacher?"
"I'm gonna be," she said, "when I finish
this PhD, which is why I'm here, to

ask you some questions." "I did go to school,"
he said, not waiting for her questions.
"Off the reservation. We were all birds.
White kids were blue birds. Some, not so smart,

got to be red birds. All us Indians
were yellow birds. I especially
remember one teacher, arithmetic.
I'd got an answer wrong. She put her face

right down in my face. I could smell her breath.
She was white. Said to me, *If I've told you
once I've told you a hundred times, that's not
how you work this problem.* So you tell me,"

the old man said, looking up with something
like a smile, "If she'd told me a hundred
times and I still didn't understand,
who do you think was the yellow bird?"

Directed by the Wind and Sun

Choirmaster

His death was the first death.
I was a child, air and muscle
Sounding for him. He shouted
Through our singing: Attack
Together   *Therefore with angels*
And archangels   Release together
And with all the company of
Heaven   Breathe after heaven
We laud and magnify thy glorious
Name   Sustain   Sustain
Evermore praising Thee and say-
Ing   I cannot remember his name,
Only his bald head beating time,
His hands chopping air into clear
Phrases, and his cremation
Holy   Holy   Holy
Lord God of Hosts
His ashes scattered from an airplane
High over the city.   *Heaven and earth*
Are full of Thy glory   And air
And breath and singing ever since
Directed by his voice: Release
Together, breathe, attack, sustain
Glory be to thee, O Lord most high
And he directed by the wind and sun
Amen.

Walking in the Cold

Some might take pleasure in discomfort,
that feeling on the face of unreasonable chill,
the painful denial of exposed earlobes. Incoming
air cleans all the way down.

But pleasure or not, we do it,
those of us who have stood by,
helpless, and watched someone who didn't,
who suffered the gradual lung-stiffening

surrender to emphysema, whose heart did
break down from the struggle to breathe, who finally
could not walk to the end of a fishing pier
or half a block in any kind of air.

Engraved on Air

Night slips up on us,
taking over the flat pond,
the broken barn, the oak tree
and swing, the front yard, the woods beyond.

Lightning bugs rise out of the ground.
You chase them long
after the light has gone. Chill
and darkness remind us children belong

in bed. You protest. When we insist,
you try to bargain:
you will be good, wash dishes,
and brush your teeth again

if we promise to let you stay up.
I promise we will, if you perform
correctly on two riddles. One:
how are lightning bugs like thunderstorms?

And two: how are thunderstorms
like you? Summer lightning flickers
slick and silent, far away.
You do not hesitate, but, quicker

than lightning bugs, have an answer:
"We can't see them in the dark
until they flash. Each one
shows us with a spark

where it is, and where
it's moved to." There is much sorrow
when you cannot solve the second riddle,
and I promise to answer it tomorrow.

Alone with your mother, I admit
that I, too, wonder
what the answer is. Lightning
closer. I hear thunder.

A lightning bug appears a foot away.
How did he get from there
to here? We navigate in darkness
and find our lives engraved on air.

Sudden thunder overhead:
close lightning shows us an unseen
farm. You cry out
in the upstairs bedroom, scream

until I get to you, hold you,
assure you everything will be all right.
Then sleep creeps up on you,
as temporary as this night.

I stroke your hair, and whisper
with the rain: your name.
All at once I understand: the answer,
Katharine, to both riddles is the same.

Home Movies

At first we believed these really were our
first steps. Then doubted. How could he have been
right there, at the exact right time? We lurched
forward and started to fall. Our father
quit filming and reached to catch us. On film,
you see me start a step. Instant cut to
me standing, unsteady, reaching for
someone you cannot see, see me start
another step. Cut to me standing,
unsteady, reaching. Cut to me standing.
You get the picture. How should I feel now,
having walked for more than half a century?
Should he have let me fall? How else could I learn?
An end to action makes a better film.

Making an Impression

Turning a page in this drawing pad,
I found a face, or the lines of a face,
pressed into the paper from something you drew,
pages and pages ago. Every line
is firm: lips like thin clouds, a rounded
triangle nose, whose sides, high, near the eyes,
refuse to join, and turn away, becoming
the airfoils of these huge eyebrows. Riding
beneath them, like small full moons, the irises
are perfect circles, with two hard dots inside.

A time will come when I am like these lines,
when you will make some gesture, say something
you've heard me say, and suddenly recognize
a ghostly drawing. I hope my lines are as true
as yours, and, when they surprise you, you will be
as delighted as I was to find this face,
to find that paper could remember
what I had long ago forgotten.

The Forgotten Child

My father chased a cloud of strange women
after his divorce. One day when I was seven,
while he was counting the fingertips on his skin,
he forgot his promise to pick me up at school.
He just forgot. When they closed the building,
I sat on my books at the corner, refusing
ride after ride, not wanting to frighten him
when he came, as I was certain he would, that
I was not there. I didn't begin to cry
until the light lessened, at first afraid
for him, and then finally for myself.

A neighbor, seeing me on the corner,
sobbing at darkness, to keep it away, insisted
on taking me home, where my frightened
and angry mother tried to comfort me with dinner,
and my father called, his regret pushing through
apology after apology, like the rush
of all those empty cars that passed my school,
not knowing they were empty, not noticing
a small child staring into their windows,
learning hard how *empty* means what it says.

The sound of rain carries memory where it will

The voice of rain on this city skylight
whispers, shouts, then settles down
to talk about my grandmother or, rather,
about sleeping at her house, where in all
innocent selfishness we children prayed
for rain, not to soak and slake tobacco
and corn in the hard fields, but to help us
sleep, by ringing on the tin roof
such a rush of voices we need not
heed, so that we were free to let
go every muscle, or curl at once
into a tight letter C, like a worm
in the sweet flesh of an ear of corn,
hidden and happy as rain to fall,
and sleep and sleep.

Sometimes in the night,
in the new, cool, quiet air,
a whip-poor-will right under the window
might wake us just enough to roll
over. In the morning, clay held
to the bottoms of our feet in layers,
and every step peeled away a small part
of the earth. Then my grandmother
made us wash our feet at the well
before we ate. I remember how cold
this water from deep under the house
and fields. I remember how clean our feet.

Kate's Birthday, Falling this Year on the Day We Change Times

You might pretend that, when you missed
the plane in Daytona Beach last week,
the airlines had already changed to Daylight
Saving Time without letting you
know, or that for the duration of Spring
Break you made your own change,
dropping back from Eastern Standard
to Nighttime Saving, and then you forgot
to reset your watch.

Officially, the hour comes out
today between Two and Three A.M.
like a cut that heals perfectly, your skin
as smooth again as the face of a lake
at sunrise, under no wind. The hour
taken while you sleep is like water
dipped from the lake in that place
standing for your birthday and poured back
in the place that stands for when you're in college
and have moved away.

Unofficially, you can take out the hour any
time the night before, so that after
eleven PM, you can move your birthday
up and start sooner being
eighteen, and not wait for the rest
of the whole country to set its clocks
ahead, you getting there first,
looking for something to eat, changing
the station, turning up the volume,
loving the music.

Casting for Air

Sometimes in dreams my father moves as full
of grace and wit as when he lived. He breathes
as if his lungs had never stiffened, laughs

the way he did before his chest tore open.
I wake up going I don't know
where, remembering his voice, almost hearing

his voice, as if the air were just still
after he said my name. I remember him then
phrasing his own songs, *Oh for a thous-*

sand tongues to sing, his brittle lungs breaking
the words on every short breath, *A may-*
zing grace, how sweet the sound. He used to fish

from an ocean pier, a trestle of raw wood
barely bridging the surf. It took him
five stops, leaning against the rail,

casting for air, to get out far enough.
Bluefish were as strong as he was. He became
a child, too excited to catch his breath.

I dream again of falling towards his voice
unbroken by the need to breathe.
I hear him say my name.

Millard Dunn is currently Professor of English, Emeritus, at Indiana University Southeast, where he taught for thirty-three years. He has also taught at Washington and Lee University and McKendree University (Kentucky Centers) and conducted creative writing workshops in the public schools of both Indiana and Kentucky and at West Texas A&M University in Canyon, Texas. In 1990 he was elected to the Indiana University Faculty Colloquium for Excellence in Teaching (FACET). In 1994 he joined four FACET colleagues to edit the first edition of *Quick Hits: Successful Strategies by Award Winning Teachers* (Bloomington: Indiana University Press). His other publications include *This Powerful Rhyme: A Workshop Approach to Shakespeare's Sonnets* (Co-authored with Ken Watson. Phoenix Education: Melbourne and Sydney, Australia, 2005).

He has held grants and fellowships from The Woodrow Wilson Foundation, Indiana University, The Kentucky Arts Council, The Kentucky Foundation for Women, and the National Endowment for the Humanities. His poetry has appeared in many literary magazines, among them *Concho River Review, Film and History, Kansas Quarterly, The Louisville Review, The Ohio Review, Poetry Northwest, Sandhills-St. Andrews Review, Shenandoah, Southern Poetry Review, Stand*, and *Tar River Poetry*. In 1983, his chapbook *Engraved on Air* won first prize in the Kentucky Arts Council Chapbook Contest and was published by the Kentucky Arts Council and the Kentucky Department of Libraries and Archives in conjunction with the Second Kentucky Writers Conference. In 1984 his poem "Directions" appeared in the *Anthology of Magazine Verse & Yearbook of American Poetry*. In 1994 his poem "Picasso's Late Drawings" won first prize for poetry in the Kentuckiana Metroversity Faculty Creative Writing Contest. His poem "Map Fragment, on Clay" has been published on a postcard by *This end up postcards*.

www.ingramcontent.com/pod-product-compliance
Lightning Source LLC
Chambersburg PA
CBHW020914090426
42736CB00008B/635